LUMINESCENCE

BY

JEEVAN BHAGWAT

LUMINESCENCE
By Jeevan Bhagwat

Cover Image:
"Photo of Night Sky"
By Tobias Bjorkli

Copyright © 2020 Jeevan Bhagwat
All rights reserved.

LUMINESCENCE
ISBN: 978-1-7327634-1-8

IN PUBLICATIONS
14 Lorraine Circle, Waban, MA 02468

DEDICATION

For Anna, of the Auroras.

ACKNOWLEDGEMENTS

Thanks to the editors at IN Publication, Joanna, Ken, and Milt, and to the editors of magazines, websites and anthologies where some of these poems first appeared: The Windsor Review, Feathertale, Kippis, Subterranean Blue Poetry, Montreal Serai, Poets Against War, Northern Cardinal Review, Tower Poetry, The Prairie Journal, The Beautiful Space, Geez Magazine, Scarborough Arts, The Ontario Poetry Society.

Thank you to Anna for her inspiration. Thank you to my parents for their love and support. Thank you to Valma and Jukka for their kindness and generosity. Finally, my love and gratitude to Devi and Jarryl for their guidance and assistance.

TABLE OF CONTENTS

PART I: DAYLIGHT   1

    THIRST   3
    OLD WOMEN, COOKING   4
    WAITING   6
    CHILDHOOD   7
    ODE TO WINTER   9
    THE SANDHILL BURIAL GROUNDS (YONGE & BLOOR)   11
    APRIL TREES   13
    ANGEL   14
    WILD WINTER SKY   16
    LAST DAY OF WINTER   17
    HOW THE LIVING CARRY THE DEAD   18
    ODE TO FORGIVENESS   20
    ODE TO SPRING   21
    THE AWAKENING   22
    WHAT THE RAIN DESIRES   23
    CRYING OVER KEATS   25
    ODE TO LOVE   27
    THE MATHEMATICS OF LOVE   29
    HELD   30
    THE TOPOGRAPHY OF LOVE   33
    CHASING COMETS   35
    AT THE SWING   37
    REQUIEM FOR LOVE   39
    THE POTTER'S WHEEL   42
    THAT NIGHT IN PARIS   44
    EPIPHANY   46
    HUMMINGBIRD   47
    (Re)BIRTH   48
    ODE TO A BUTTERFLY   49
    ODE TO TIME   51
    ON HER FAVOURITE COFFEE MUG   53
    MY MOTHER, WALKING HOME FROM WORK   54

PART II: TWILIGHT   55

- OIL SPILL   57
- THE ARRIVAL   58
- THE INSATIABLE HUNGER   60
- UPROOTED   61
- TOMORROW'S CHILD   63
- CHURCH   65
- DRIVING TO LAS VEGAS   66
- LONE GULL   68
- THE INTERRACIAL LOVERS   70
- SCARBOROUGH – A LOVE POEM   71
- ODE TO BEAUTY   77
- THE LANGUAGE OF BIRDS   79
- ATTAWAPISKAT   81
- CARDED   86
- TORONTO   87
- THE LAND OF PLENTY   90
- TRANSCENDENCE   92
- HUMANITY, LOST   93
- CONCRETE DREAM   95
- FINCH   96
- ODE TO A ROBIN   98
- THE MURMURATION   99
- NOTHING FOR GRANTED   100
- THE LINDEN TREE   101
- ISA AND THE SPIDER   103
- WISHING WELL PARK   104

PART I: DAYLIGHT

THIRST

All day

I slithered through the city

zigzagging, restless

as a rattlesnake. Water

cannot slake my thirst

when sunlight blisters speech,

and my tongue unfurls

like a strip of highway

licking its way to the sea.

Words are cactus needles,

stitching together my

parched lips,

when all I want is

to speak my heart,

and quench this desire

for you.

OLD WOMEN, COOKING

They are always there

at family gatherings,

scarcely noticed

on the heart's periphery

cooking and preparing,

talking amongst themselves

in foreign tongues

unknown to hungry ears.

Dressed in black with

covered heads,

they shift with the grace and

patience of seasons,

their ankles thick and

strong as oaks

rooted in traditions of time.

These old women with their

wise, dark eyes

they churn their pots in

secret rhythms,

and spin the earth

on its axis of time,

flavouring our lives with history.

WAITING

You say it hurts to sit

so instead, you stand

staring out the windows that have

become your eyes. Ever since he

packed his bags and drove his pickup

down the road's long stretch

of asphalt tongue, taking with him

your dreams of fourteen years,

your re-kindled heart, your last

chance at holding on to something

in this world where life is a game

of straws, you stand

waiting; like a house

on its foundations

longing to be entered, like

an empty rocking chair

shaking with expectation,

your eyes fixed on the

distant horizon,

somewhere beyond the heart's

hopeful light.

CHILDHOOD

I'm not quite sure how it happened,

when it all unraveled like

a bicycle's chain

to a reference point

for lost youth.

The summer seemed to last forever,

beneath skies draped in

a satin blue,

when Time was young

and the hours oozed like

molasses from an old tin jar.

How we laughed and played

in the golden sunlight,

our shadows moving on the green,

between transitions of

day and night,

and boy and man

it seemed.

With outstretched arms we glided,

the silent schoolyard left behind,

as bicycles whizzed

past empty swing sets

and curfews on grown up dreams.

ODE TO WINTER

Sad composer of the season,

no bright eyed daisies

dance to your tunes,

no bluebirds

ever sing your songs.

Alone and neglected

by the dreamers of Spring,

you haunt the frozen landscape

inscribing your name

in calligraphies of frost

upon our window panes.

But there is yet tenderness

to be found in your music,

yet beauty

in your symphonies of snow,

though the north wind moans

like a soft, slow cello

to the rattling applause

of the trees.

THE SANDHILL BURIAL GROUNDS (YONGE & BLOOR)

This is the spot

where the wind wails most,

where the past and present

intersect

into a strange cacophony

of myriad sounds.

Those who cross here

speak of the wind

with a certain kind of

reluctant respect,

as if it pierces through you

like a Sandhill spear,

to keep you from

this sacred soil.

But the wind remembers

the thunder of drums,

and ancient songs

from ancestral tongues,

knows the underlying

spirit of the land

reverberates

through its furious throat,

when on any given day

old bones rattle

from deep beneath

the city's asphalt skin,

where buried under

paved sediments of time,

these arteries

still bleed ghosts.

APRIL TREES

Silhouetted against a slice of sky

pale effigies in emperor's clothes

slowly awaken to Spring's caress,

their branches beseeching

the hallowed heavens

for benedictions of birdsong

and rain.

ANGEL

(For My Mother)

It had been so long

since my last visit

and, wanting to surprise you

I found you outside,

your basket of linen

half full on the lawn,

your sheets swaying on the line.

You are singing softly

in the cool of evening,

an Ave Maria as tender

and sweet

as the memory of childhood

when at your feet,

I listened

for the very first time.

And you turn and smile

in the shimmering light,

heart as pure as heavenly love,

while all around you

white sheets gleam,

like angel wings

unfolding.

WILD WINTER SKY

Wild winter sky

broods on the horizon,

perched up high

with outstretched wings,

watching, waiting

to swoop down swiftly

and pierce its talons

into your dreams of spring.

Wild winter sky

shows no mercy,

shatters your will

to defy its cold,

freezes your desire

for the warmth of summer,

and leaves you dreamless

in its frosty hold.

LAST DAY OF WINTER

At first

we are confused,

unsure what to make of it,

this coagulation of light

that seeps through a tear

in the fabric of sky,

how it colours our faces

and illuminates the fields

where the first, shy crocuses sprout;

and then, the realization

that hits us with the force

of a robin's song,

now on its deathbed, bleeding

who knew Winter's blood

could feel this warm?

HOW THE LIVING CARRY THE DEAD

We carry them in the early

morning hours,

through the glimmer of dawn

into the world of the living

which they have now left

behind.

Throughout the day they

inhabit us,

move within our bodies

in a weightless desire

to fill their need

for gravity.

Sometimes we see them

in the faces of strangers,

in a smile or gesture

familiar to our eyes

and then, in an instant

they are gone again,

always leaving us with

the wretched heaviness of loss

our hearts must inevitably bear

At night

we take them with us to bed,

offer prayers to the heavens

and patiently await

their arrival in the spirit

landscape of our dreams,

this is how we carry them

from their past to the present

and into our future,

with every step

we take in grief,

with every strand

 of memory,

for that which we bury

our love exhumes.

ODE TO FORGIVENESS

It is a seed we plant

within ourselves,

that sprouts and grows

and pushes through

the sediment of guilt

weighing us down,

till in a moment of

self-redemption,

it breaks through the surface

of the hardened heart,

to bloom and breathe

its freedom.

ODE TO SPRING

Vernal contractions

awaken the earth,

as water breaks from

gathering clouds,

and baby buds birth

into bundles of joy,

delivered by the hands

of Spring.

THE AWAKENING

Shadows of maples

stretch across the street,

their gnarled fingers

scratching the dawn

while somewhere, high

in the leafless canopy

a cardinal sings a cappella,

his notes, tap dancing

in three quarter rhythm,

awakening the city

to Spring.

WHAT THE RAIN DESIRES

What the rain desires most

is the body,

it seeps through your clothing

ever so subtly,

with long, wet fingers

searching to find

the surface of skin

and bone.

The rain has no time

for apologies,

when you run from its reach

for the shelter of trees,

or shut your windows

in a desperate attempt

to keep it from

getting inside,

for the rain is drenched

in fantasies of flesh,

wants more than anything

to trickle down,

and trace the topography

of your covered torso,

the curvature of muscle

and spine.

The rain is a

jealous lover,

dampening your will

against its advance,

whispering *you're mine*

into your ear

before you break free

from its grasp.

It follows you home

till you step inside,

and winks at you

from every street puddle,

letting you know its

wet intention,

to never let its love

go dry.

CRYING OVER KEATS

A thing of beauty is a joy for ever – John Keats

You love watching the stars

in the Milky Way,

their fiery brilliance

a Polaroid picture

developing before your eyes.

On those crisp Autumn evenings

beneath the negative film of night,

I read you Keats

while you cried in my arms,

the Chinese lanterns

all around us,

soft fallen kites on the grass.

You asked,

could a thing of beauty

be a joy forever?

as we sat together

beneath the sequined sky,

our wondering eyes

gazing up

at those first bright sparks

and the birth of stars,

still glimmering

across oceans of time.

ODE TO LOVE

We feel you

in the first bright

spark of life

when, trembling with fear

our voices cry out

for the comfort of our

mothers' touch.

In the early days

when time is young

and we grow into

our bodies and minds,

you come to us

bewildering our hearts

with new sensations

we struggle to define.

Your fire engulfs us

in the prime of our years,

hoping to transform

the conscience within,

to a synthesis of being

strong enough,

to resist the antithesis

of hate.

When twilight dawns and

our days grow short,

we reap the harvest

of family and friends,

and see you sparkle

through the vista of years

as our journey approaches

its end.

And when our eyes

at last close shut,

there is yet a glimmer

to light our way,

back to the beginning

from where we started,

back into the hands

of You.

THE MATHEMATICS OF LOVE

You say that once

we were singular souls,

denominators unto ourselves,

that alone in our oneness

this life seemed nothing more

than a dice roll

of probability and chance.

Now our lives

are two halves of

a whole,

the unfolding of our love,

a straight line marking

the shortest distance

between two random hearts.

HELD

Though we all expected it

prepared for it,

the day I got the news

that she was gone

it hit me hard, harder

than a slap from a

jilted lover, or the

harsh realization that life

can sometimes be so

devastatingly unfair,

so fragile and oh,

so brief.

I was young then, too young

to think of mortality,

of missed phone calls and

unspoken words,

of all the letters that

went unopened,

and second chances that were

no more.

A numbness seeped into me,

flowed through my veins

making frozen the body,

till my lungs constrained

beneath the weight of loss,

and like a wounded animal

relying on instinct,

I sought refuge

at the foot of your door.

Looking back, I had no right

no right to burden you with this

you, whose love I had forsaken,

whose trust, I could not keep.

With a mouth full of silence

I choked on my heart,

unable to articulate

the gravity of my pain.

But you held me in your arms

when evening's last lights

were fading in the sky,

and winter hushed the city

with a soft

forgiving snow.

You held me in your arms

when the night wept jewelled stars,

and the wind wailed like

a banshee

at the threshold of your door.

In the golden glow of morning

I marvelled at your hands,

their small and tender palms

capable of such strength,

such fortitude of love

to hold another's heart,

when it was bruised

and falling.

THE TOPOGRAPHY OF LOVE

To the hill's high summit

the trail winds serpentine

through treacherous terrain

as far as the heart can see.

Steadfast we hike, courage in tote,

the looseness of gravel

beneath our boots,

a constant reminder to

keep our vigilance

when the underneath is

sometimes lacking.

Now and then

couples pass us by,

the young, holding hands

in an awkward gait,

the old, ascending with

surer strides

back to their journey's beginning.

We give and take in this

joint adventure,

each trying to navigate

the topography of our love,

while we forge ahead

with a shared faith

in synchronous strides

to where the trail ends,

and opens up

like a trusting heart

into a space

we both can enter.

CHASING COMETS

Uncle Harry grabs his binoculars

and heads out into the cold

autumn night. Six months ago,

doctors told him his prostate

had blossomed into a ripe avocado,

tests had to be done

the diagnosis,

inconclusive.

Now, every night at 10 o'clock

he steps out of his shadow

into the light of distant stars,

leaving behind his

malignant fears,

to search for comet ISON.

Belched out from the Oort cloud

on a wing and a prayer

trajectory to the sun,

he swears he's seen its

neon tail, a gleaming teardrop

across night's ebon cheek.

The astronomers predict its demise, but

Uncle Harry scoffs at them,

hoping against all odds

the old boy survives

to fly another day.

On a dark November evening

ISON brushes the sun,

Uncle Harry looks up

for a glimmer of hope

when the doctors confirm

no sign of cancer.

A day later, astronomers gasp

as a faint dot streams

past the glittering globe,

tail blazing stubbornly

through the starry ether.

AT THE SWING

Pushing you on a swing,

your hair glazed in a

honeyed light,

as you turn my way

and smile at me,

rejoicing in the freedom

of flight.

I recall you mentioning

how love is a gift

our hearts receive

only for a moment in time;

that how, someday

we must let it go

to find its way into others.

But in this life of

give and take

where every moment becomes

our past,

I'll celebrate the gift

I found in you,

knowing that for now

with every swing,

Love pushes you back

to me.

REQUIEM FOR LOVE

1

I step off the 85 bus

into the unforgiving winter wind

and trudge my way

through a shroud of snow.

2

You are sitting on a

park bench, waiting

your pale face cracked

in the evening light,

like a heart crumbling

beneath the weight of remorse.

3

I sit beside you

tongueless as the trees,

your indifferent hand

held loosely in mine,

and we speak no words

to eulogize our loss

but together,

mourn the death of love.

THE POTTER'S WHEEL

Night sky spinning,

a brilliant umbrella of stars

their beauty burning into us

across centuries of space and time.

In this vast expanse of universe,

there is neither a *here* nor *there*

no single point of reference

to guide the questioning soul,

only the certainty that you exist

for reasons unknown to you.

On a bright, blue pebble

hurtling through the void

eventually,

you come to realize

that we too are part

of an incalculable number

fashioned and forged

out of stardust and light

by an act of love

that emboldens the spirit,

and moulds our humanity

on the Potter's wheel.

THAT NIGHT IN PARIS

I remember little else of that evening

at Chez Maurice, the Paris skyline

a gaudy tapestry of

sequined stars and neon lights.

Was it overindulgence of the Pinot-noir?

What was the year – 1999? Or perhaps

The dare-you-to-try escargot?

It simply refused to go down.

Four hours later in the ER

Nurse Attitude scoffed at the sight

of another tourist unaccustomed

to the delicacies of French cuisine.

I remember the way she glared at me

Parlez-vous Francais? Non?

(my stomach spinning out of control

at the scent of sterilized floors).

I remember the doctor talking to you –

your words, *food poisoning,* barely audible,

a prescription being filled, an old

wheelchair groaning beneath my weight,

and all those forms surrendered to

Nurse Attitude; and you, laughing

as my stomach, in defiance,

empties to her grumpy *merci.*

EPIPHANY

I don't profess to know

what Love is,

all my life I've tried in vain

to unlock its mystery

and figure it out,

never once coming close

to succeeding,

but this much I know;

whenever you turn to me

and smile,

your eyes, blue fireflies

hovering in flight,

all logic slips

from the mind's grasp,

and all my defences

come undone,

till I am left with nothing

but this simple truth:

Love is an epiphany of the heart.

HUMMINGBIRD

My tongue is a hummingbird

that nightly visits

your pink petals

in search of nectar.

Clasp me close

to your blushing blooms,

let me taste

your liquid love.

(Re)BIRTH

Gracefully, beautifully

you open unto me

till my eyes burn

with the purity of your love.

Naked,

I tremble

as a newborn child,

you receive me

and wrap me

in brand new skin,

my heart ignites

and I breathe again,

oh Love

I breathe again.

ODE TO A BUTTERFLY

You were nothing more

than a little dot

when first I saw you

on the underside of a leaf,

your yoke of promise

a precious pearl,

sparkling in the summer sun.

All week

reports of machines

tearing into the earth's brown flesh,

fracking for oil

in the name of greed,

headlined the daily news.

Our appetite blossomed

much like your own

when, as a caterpillar

you gorged yourself

on all my prized lilies.

That day when I watched you

emerge from your cocoon

transformed into a creature

of beauty and light,

I wondered at our own

metamorphosis of mind,

if we'll ever transcend

our need for greed,

as you took to flight

for the very first time,

on gossamer wings and

a prayer.

ODE TO TIME

In the beginning,

you grab hold of us

and seize us by the wrist,

your texture, rough

as granules of sand

that eventually seep through

our fingers.

We scoff at mortality

in the prime of youth

our days, stretching out

into a seeming forever,

when hours are long

and the years, longer.

But in the end, we seek

to feel you again

though you run like a river

through our memories and dreams,

your texture, slippery

as water flowing

out of the palms of our hands.

Perhaps you are nothing

but a construct of the mind,

an invention born

of our imagination;

but to live is to feel you

in the atoms of our being,

a constant companion

who urges us forth

into the promise

of our own becoming.

ON HER FAVOURITE COFFEE MUG

Every time she presses her lips

against your cold, hard exterior,

leaving imprints of lipstick

red upon your brim;

every time she drinks you

into her,

her soft tongue sweetened

with her favourite tea,

I steam with jealousy

wanting only to hold you

and shatter your (s)mugness

to pieces.

MY MOTHER, WALKING HOME FROM WORK

Every day on the slick

 salt strewn street,

Winter's long tongue

of snow and ice,

your distant image rises up

against the howling rage of winds,

the freezing rain,

the stinging cold,

your brave heart shining

against the odds,

all in the name

of love.

PART II: TWILIGHT

OIL SPILL

In the news

another leaky pipeline

is bursting at its seams,

but this time, nowhere near

a neon metropolis and

its coal consuming citizens,

but beyond the concrete and steel

that encase our synthetic dreams,

past the last stretch

of asphalt, to where the land

sinks back to field, to river

to humble beginnings,

where innocence

is a new born hatchling

diving head first into

our flowing ignorance.

THE ARRIVAL

Little refugee boy

steps off the plane

unto a tarmac of

snow and ice,

feels the north wind's kiss

cold upon his cheeks,

now red as a

Canadian berry.

In this land of possibilities

he will dare to dream again,

dare to reimagine

a future without fear,

and plant his roots to flourish

in new and tolerant soil.

He takes a deep breath

and walks towards the airport

his parents, by his side

guiding him on,

as he smiles and sticks his tongue out

to catch a falling snowflake

and savour the sweet taste

of freedom.

THE INSATIABLE HUNGER

Run off from chemical plant

seeps into soil,

sinks its way deep down strata

where the earth gives way

to water.

Day after day

we grow obese

on this destructive diet

of fossil fuels,

while far from our conscience

a river bleeds black

where mallards are motionless

on the surface of grief,

their wing beats, silenced

by the ooze of oil.

UPROOTED

I didn't ask to come here,

didn't ask to be

uprooted

from my island home,

and displaced in this land

of snow.

Transplanted,

I ache to blossom

in this alien soil,

this frozen domain,

where even the rain

is cold.

My brown face

stains

this white landscape,

and like a weed

I'm kept in check,

never to flourish

in this foreign earth,

never to inherit

this field.

TOMORROW'S CHILD

Come child

let me teach you peace

for you know too much

of war and despair,

too much

of hunger and pain.

Let me teach you

how to love again,

that one day

you will have the strength

to shield your heart

from hate.

Let me teach you

how to trust again,

that one day

you will not place faith

in those who preach

with guns.

Come child

and embrace tomorrow,

for the dream of

peace

lives in you.

CHURCH

You are my church

in you, I taste God,

am absolved of my sins

and become redeemed

in the light of your

stained glass eyes.

Lead me to the alter of your heart,

have me recite

the liturgy of Love

and quench my thirst

with your lips' sweet wine.

Come feed my soul

with the bread that is your body,

let me find salvation

in the thrusts of grace

that unfold from our

sacred love.

DRIVING TO LAS VEGAS

Lonely hitchhiker

by the side of the road,

a mirage of contradictions

to my tired eyes,

as I pick her up

and hurtle forth

into the deep, dark mouth of night.

A red haired Rockette

or Broadway dancer,

I hardly know

what to make of him,

her Maybelline eyes

adorned in mascara,

the Adam's apple under

his chin.

She lights up a menthol

and tells me how

this is his last chance to shine,

to make it big

in this neon jungle

where dreams are dice

we roll.

I say I'm gonna get rich,

she winks, he smiles

and I keep on driving,

three travellers embarked

on a journey of chance

born of our crisscrossed dreams.

LONE GULL

No one knew you

not even your name,

no one seemed to care

that, day after day

you would sit outside

in the unforgiving cold,

hand extended in a pleading gesture

asking for alms

without words.

The suits passed you by

unacknowledged,

your disheveled hair

casting shadows on your face

invisible

to their sightless eyes.

When the ambulance came

that December day

and took your frozen body

away,

the street corner seemed

more empty,

a space with no face

to remember you by,

You,

a lone gull

tired of hovering

just beyond

our collective conscience.

THE INTERRACIAL LOVERS

What does it matter

that they've bordered our desire?

That they've refused our tongues

of the bitter sweet longing

in our mouths?

They crucify our pride

and drown our dreams

but sacrificed,

we will rise above their ignorance

and find redemption

in the colours of our love.

SCARBOROUGH – A LOVE POEM

1.

Your face

is a map of the world,

a welcoming beacon

that smiles upon

every newcomer

in search of a home.

Your voice

is a river of accents,

singing in the dialects

of foreign tongues

that resound with pride

in our ears.

Your beauty

is in your diversity,

in your ethnic neighbourhoods

where colours combine

like rainbows that bleed

into one.

Your strength

is in your people,

whose myriad cultures

intertwine

to define your

Canadian soul.

2.

I have always loved you.

In the early days

when I came to you

as a child removed

from my island home,

you welcomed me with

open arms,

and set my feet

upon your soil

to plant my roots

and grow.

At the apartment buildings

on Birchmount Road,

I learned to play hockey,

made friends and cheered

the Maple Leafs on

with every slap shot goal,

and at Walt's Variety

on the corner of St. Clair,

I wasted my teenage days away,

when Time was an hourglass

filled with sand,

and the future was

a far off dream.

3.

When the 70's dawned

you were the new Suburbia,

a magnet for industry

where shopping malls

popped up like dandelions

on pristine lots,

and cash flowed out

like liquid concrete

into the foundations of

factory plants.

Life was good back then,

as communities grew with

immigrant families

eager to find a home.

But the politicians came and

amalgamated you,

the downtowners complained and

ghettoized you,

the media raged and

criminalized you,

till your name was

slandered and soiled.

They never saw

the beauty within you,

where mom and pop stores

peopled street corners,

and backyard barbeques

on warm summer nights

spoke of different cultures

that came together

to learn and grow

as one.

They were blind

to your natural splendour,

to your limestone Bluffs

that climb the sky,

and your lush, green parks

where childhood memories

of campfire stories

on marshmallow nights

live on in the dreams

of my heart.

Let them have their condos

and office towers,

their rush hour traffic

on car clogged streets,

their 24/7 rat race lives

in cities that never sleep.

I'll take your quiet neighbourhoods and parks

and the multiethnic faces

that colour your streets,

for my heart is a song

that resounds in your name,

and I will always and forever

love you.

ODE TO BEAUTY

In ancient days you were revered

and honoured with temples far and wide,

the virgin choirs sang for you

at every dawn and eventide;

the white robed priests burned incense sweet

and mouthed their incantation prayers

with sacrifice of slaughtered sheep

to appease Olympian ears;

then grey bearded bards took to their quills

with imaginations wild and free,

while worshippers of your name rejoiced

and called you, Aphrodite.

But gone are those days of long ago

and ruined, those temples of prayer and song,

the gods are dead and now usurped

by an arrogant, human throng.

Ravaged is the land by man's machines

and polluted with oil is the sea,

our consciousness retards while we are bound

to capitalism's decree.

Gone are those bards who recited your name

gone, your alters of flowers,

we sacrificed you in the name of profit

while greed of our wisdom, devours.

Then let me be your vessel to sing anew

songs and rhymes for a wired age,

invoke our psyche to yet break free

from the dark confines of this mental cage,

and when at last, the veil of ignorance

is lifted from humanity's sight,

inspire us to see beyond the glare

of our own synthetic light;

and when the Poet's mantra sounds

to breathe life into you again,

let your resurrection be

the death of Greed and Profit's reign.

THE LANGUAGE OF BIRDS

Once, we were neighbours

eons ago,

shared the trees with them

when we dared not venture

to walk upon

solid ground.

They brought sweet music

to our songless hearts,

taught us to listen

to the rhythms of rain

when all we could hear

was the thunder's tongue.

We understood them then,

their language of song

inspiring our voices

to rise above

the guttural grunts

of our speech.

Now they watch us

from chain sawed trees,

the foolish primates

who only learned

the language of profit and greed.

ATTAWAPISKAT

Among tiny houses that lie scattered

like spilled pills from a child's hand,

the gravel road stretches, deep into

Attawapiskat's hollowed heart.

Here, the wind blows

without the comfort of song,

its tongue, crushed

by the weight of wails

resounding from mothers whose

rivers of tears

are the only clean water around.

She walks out to the edge of town

where the road uncoils like a captive snake

slithering its way to freedom.

One day, she'll leave this place behind

and run as far as she can dream,

away from the alcohol and drugs,

away from the helplessness

that binds her to this land.

One day, she'll give it all up

turn her back on her past,

take off her shoes,

and learn to run free on ice.

The elders warn

watch your step in these parts,

lest your feet get cut

on broken dreams,

but sooner or later

everyone here bleeds,

everyone limps

in this frozen limbo.

Nothing grows in this infertile soil

nothing blooms anymore.

In the crowded cemetery, she walks among

tombstones with familiar names,

brings flowers for her sister

who sleeps in the earth,

with a long, white dress

and slit wrists.

The young find no hope

for a better tomorrow,

when neglect is a word

harder than a fist

and deeper than the bottom

of a bootlegged beer bottle,

where their sorrows never drown

but instead, learn to swim.

Drugs and booze

puncture their dreams

and weave through the fabric

of this small, northern town,

stitching together

a communal shroud

that binds their heavy hearts

in grief.

Tired of the emptiness

that fills her from within,

she reaches for a bottle

of pink painkiller pills,

pops the lid open

and swallows them all

before closing her brown eyes

forever.

Poverty lives here;

gets gift wrapped with a big

shiny bow, and passed down

to succeeding generations,

till it dwells in the

empty pockets of parents,

who can never pay the price tag

affixed to their child's dreams.

Despair haunts here;

it inhabits the burnt out eyes

of weary men and women,

coagulates in their throats

to a thick, unswallowable lump

that chokes away resilience

and mutes their anguished cries

to a barely audible whimper

unheard by Ottawa's ears.

On the road heading out of Attawapiskat

she leaves behind her empty dreams,

unlaces her shoes and takes them off,

and for the first time

in her sixteen years,

she is running on gravel and ice.

CARDED

Policeman stops me at Jane&Finch

says he needs to get some info,

policeman stops me 'cuz my skin

ain't white like Toronto snow.

He takes my name, number and other details

filling me with unease,

pencils me on to his little card

with the other minorities.

Government eyes me with distrust

wants to know about my *kind,*

gathers statistics and sifts through them

to see what they can find.

Policeman ends the interrogation

his curiosity now satisfied,

thanks me for my *cooperation*

and walks away with my pride.

TORONTO

I step out of the cab

and into her arms,

as she spreads out like

spider webs in all directions,

weaving through different

ethnic enclaves

that together, strand her DNA.

Liberal in outlook

and young at heart,

she is a new Jerusalem

for the modern age,

where mosque and synagogue

stand undivided

to worship without walls

or fear.

Italian, Indian

and everyone in between,

carve their identity

into her asphalt flesh,

a kaleidoscope of cultures

coming together

into one shared dream of peace.

Mouths collide

into a symphony of speech

born from the dialects

of un-English tongues,

whose twang and accent

transforms her voice

into a synthesis of myriad sounds.

Black faces,

white faces,

interracial skin,

open my eyes

to an aesthetic of being

freed from the prejudice of the past

and the dogma of colonial ideals.

I watch as she yawns

at Dundas Square,

and blinks her bright lit

billboard eyes,

waiting for tomorrow

when the future unfolds

to ignite

her millennial dreams.

THE LAND OF PLENTY

In the land of plenty

stomachs groan

to symphonies of want

outside the food banks

that cannot wean

the hungry

on hope alone.

Politicians play saviours

and smile for the cameras,

make campaign promises

they cannot keep,

then vote themselves

a wage increase

on the backs of the

working poor.

Here, single mothers swim

in rivers of debt,

watch their children struggle

to stay afloat

on welfare cheques

that cannot buy

a sail to hoist their dreams.

In the land of plenty

the poor slip through

a conscience cracked,

become forgotten

to the fortunate few,

become the faces of me

and you.

TRANSCENDENCE

This tremulous untethering of life

from the body's mould of matter,

this silencing of the senses

that unfolds in our last breath,

though fundamental and fearful

to nature and to man,

invokes the evolution

of consciousness and being

as the spirit transcends

this corpus clay

on its journey towards Truth

and Love.

HUMANITY, LOST

Sometime

in a not too distant future,

when the sun has scorched the land,

and the ice caps have melted

into a liquid memory,

and we have all but doomed ourselves

to a dinosaur destiny,

who would believe

we inhabited this earth?

This lost paradise

we once called home?

I think of Voyager

on its one way trip

to the blurred out edges

of our interstellar dreams,

what story would it tell

were it intercepted

by some far away

alien world?

Would Bach's Brandenburg concerto

still sound as sweet?

Or the echo of our voices

recall our hopes and fears?

Would what we've bequeathed

ever truly convey

the essence

of our lost humanity?

CONCRETE DREAM

City swells

to the horizon's edge,

while condo canopies

blot out sun

till all that remains

is a memory of sky.

At night,

birds break their necks

on windows,

their lifeless bodies

littering pavement

to greet us each

sombre morn.

But the cranes come and go

building towers of glass

and recycled steel,

till our lives are encased

in a concrete dream

that hardens our desire

for sprawl.

FINCH

Am I to believe

that amidst the cacophony

of man and machine,

the trees yet listen

to your ancient songs?

You come to me in a dream,

a gift of feathers

floating down

to sing the earth back

to life

while I,

a creature of flesh and bone

destined to dust

in this corpus clay

am now become

an awakened spirit,

a Lazarus

to your cadenced call.

ODE TO A ROBIN

If I could dissect your song

what wonders would I find therein?

What chords composed

by a consciousness divine

to awaken our hearts

to love?

Your voice burns symphonies

into my soul,

and like a hatchling breaking free,

my spirit transcends

this mortal shell

in search of truth

and beauty.

THE MURMURATION

And then,

in a moment of wild abandonment,

an epiphany emerged

from the starlings' murmuration,

where out of the rapturous

choreography of life

the geometry of Beauty

revealed itself,

and I beheld

the imprint of God.

NOTHING FOR GRANTED

Never take for granted
the day that's given you,
life is but an hourglass
whose grains of sand are few.

The precious present moment
is all we've really got,
yesterday came and went
tomorrow well may not.

There is no looking forward
there is no looking back,
only the here and now
on every traveller's track.

But if, by intuition
you feel there's something more,
look up and let your faith
find what you're searching for.

THE LINDEN TREE

Your loveliness took root

inside me,

branched its way through my body

till my spirit cried out

with an aria of

linden leaves.

All this time

you watched over me,

ringed my years with

dendrochronology,

while my sapling dreams sprouted

and grew.

Lovers came and went,

friends disappeared,

but always, there was you

steadfast and true,

who oxygenated my lungs

when hope was hard

to breathe.

When the dark shadow comes

to cut me down

in the twilight of my days to be,

know that you carved

your name on my heart,

and filled my life

with beauty.

ISA AND THE SPIDER

In a tiny apartment

above ground,

Isa sits in his armchair

and stares out the window

daydreaming of the homestead

and Valma's blue eyes,

while next to his coffee

bitter-sweetened with time,

spider stands silent

spinning strands of web,

to weave his past together

and catch his long lost dreams.

WISHING WELL PARK

For Jarryl

Do you remember those golden days

when we were young and free?

We walked together in Wishing Well Park

immersed in greenery.

The summer seemed to last forever

beneath a sky of ocean blue,

we watched as clouds sailed by like ships

and vanished from our view.

We laughed and played as brothers do

while Time itself grew old,

the seasons changed till summer's warmth

gave way to winter's cold.

Now those days have gone away

but oh, that we could be

together again in Wishing Well Park,

when we were young and free.

ABOUT THE POET

Jeevan Bhagwat is a Scarborough poet who has been published widely in literary journals, anthologies and websites across Canada, the U.S. and internationally. In 2003 and 2005, he was awarded the Monica Ladell Prize for Poetry by the Scarborough Arts Council and in 2015 he was the recipient of the Scarborough Urban Hero Award for Arts and Culture. In 2012 his poetry book, The Weight of Dreams was published by IN Publications. He is the co-founder of The Scarborough Poetry Club and a member of The League of Canadian Poets.

www.ingramcontent.com/pod-product-compliance
Lightning Source LLC
Chambersburg PA
CBHW031452040426
42444CB00007B/1068